THRASH

THRASH

Michael Diebert

Brick Road Poetry Press
www.brickroadpoetrypress.com

Copyright © 2022 by Michael Diebert

Cover photo: © Marcinwarmia - stock.adobe.com

Author photo: © 2022 by Rosalind Staib

Library of Congress Control Number: 2022936649
ISBN: 978-1-950739-08-0

Published by Brick Road Poetry Press
341 Lee Road 553
Phenix City, AL 36867
www.brickroadpoetrypress.com

Brick Road logo by Dwight New

ALL RIGHTS RESERVED
Printed in the United States of America

Table of Contents

I

Jazzercise...5
Marriage..7
In Your Teaching Dream...9
Hopkinsville..10
The Miracle Worker...11
Three Storms..13
In Your Eggshell Dream..18
Our Twenties..20
The oncologist, hand on the doorknob,..........................22
New Glasses..23

II

Thesis...27
Chemo..28
The Mirage..33
In the Lobby of the Women's Residence.........................34
Harbor Island..36
In Your Flea Market Dream..37
Royal Caribbean...39
Coupling..40
The Saloon in the Side of the Mountain..........................41
In Your Teaching Dream...43
Into History..44

III

Eastman Meditations...49
Thrash..61
Autumn..63
What I Fell Into..64
The Class of '86..65
While Everyone Else Was Disappearing..........................67
Make It Easy on Yourself..68
First Friday..70

IV

On the Rapids..75
Franklin County Lowdown...76

Second Act	78
Letter to Ferris from Decatur	82
In Your Teaching Dream	83
Trash Duty	84
Three-Mushroom Tart, Dayton, Oregon	85
Remission	86
Two Raptures	88
Repair	91
I woke up and I was a comforter	93
Notes	95
Acknowledgments	97
About the Author	100

*I talked with unusual briskness
and sharp enunciation because
I knew I must be a vigorous adult
with a major problem just one room away.*

   —Mark Halliday

*when I have been suffering at times I could
step away from it by embracing it, a blues thing,
a John Donne thing, divest by wrestling, then sing.*

   —Diane Seuss

I

Jazzercise

In a room brimming with women, you are the only man.
You pull out moves you never have before—
hold in your core, chassé right
into a back ball change, plié over
a hypothetical garden hose,
try to stay invested, keep a serious face,
keep your arms above your heart.
The instructor pauses mid-hip walk,
says *put on some makeup, I can't see you.*
You feel your pocket. Your wallet
is nonexistent. Your water bottle
is an unsculpted block of marble.
You bounce outside on a medicine ball
and decide you need a hammer
to throttle that pesky worm in your ear.
In the pattering rain, in the blear
of streetlights, an Ace materializes.
You march past the riding mowers,
wave off the overalled clerks,
bypass the siding, the overhead lighting,
reach the back counter where new metal
is ground, where the must is strongest.
You try to describe your key
from memory. The woman throws up her hands
and says *I'm not an artist.* A cuckoo
emerges from a gingerbread house.
You cough and you're in the stacks
lifting a book about a book about working out.
Toilet flushing—no, child slurping
a chocolate malted through a straw,

regarding you from a rocking chair,
your football knees and marching band feet.
You're listing to the right. You flip
reckless through the five-thousand-plus pages
in hopes of an illustration.

Marriage

The memory slaps his face
like seawater, and he shudders:

years ago, in a different persona,
steering the hatchback

down some county road,
passing tobacco barns, sensing

there never would be a house
or a woman to keep him around,

total control, therefore no point
in feeling anything but good.

He exits the interstate,
sees three saplings

planted in the median, green limbs
straining toward the sun, bees

murmuring and drunk on their mission.
It takes his breath. So much so

he pulls into the church parking lot
to await his breath's return.

A long time he lived by himself.
These days, he and his wife

go to lots of celebrations
with lots of food and familiarity,

and he often sits off to the side
oohing and aahing,

sometimes just nodding,
and he's grateful and content

to be ensconced, to see time
both behind and in front of him.

He recites this under his breath.
When newlyweds burst from the sanctuary

and run through a shower of birdseed,
he rolls down his window

and cheers the loudest of anyone.
Then, another feeling

and another vision, a strange one:
a man in a leather jacket,

motorcycle helmet under his arm,
sunglasses, stubbled chin,

stubborn jaw, standing in the middle
of a bed of pink and red azaleas,

water can in hand, not quite
himself, not quite not.

In Your Teaching Dream

Twenty-two students and the cat in your bedroom.
The brainiac lolls on the beanbag chair.
You mumble something about the need for research.
Roll book, lesson plan, posture: forgotten.
The room feels full of marshmallows
or just a lot of lukewarm water.
Everyone has to use the bathroom, two at a time.
The troublemakers from world lit
are rifling your bureau and arguing
who has the best chicken strips.
You seem to remember a project was due.
Sam Cunningham, who sat next to you in band,
walks in and tries to give you his journal.
You say it's late. He smiles,
lays it down and walks out. On the cover is a clown.
Let's try again tomorrow, you say.
Everyone scatters. Not a book to be seen.
Someone's left an Etch-a-Sketch on your shelf.
You shake it once or twice. The maraca inside.
A woodpecker jackhammers the house.
You run out, throw a suitcase at the roof.
No bird. The rattling moves to the hedge,
the mailbox, up the predawn street.
You've never left this lawn in your life.
You step off the curb into a fusillade of eggs.

Hopkinsville

Town outside time, smug, self-satisfied.
Tobacco browning. Amish buggies kicking up dust.
Quiet neighbors. Dead mall. Three Chinese buffets
in the same half-mile. Mill grinding around the clock.
I didn't want to make it work. Bigger things awaited.
Yet it sticks to my dreams. I persist
in believing I left behind something shiny.
Friends, you met there, got married and stayed there.
You drove five hours to see me get married,
drove back that night. Did that happen?
That's been forever. I know you were here,
you're in this picture from the reception
decked out in black and lavender. I'm sorry
I didn't stay at your table, you know how it goes,
you're skating on the surface, you don't see people,
I mean you do but you're circling so fast.
I wanted to be funny and dumb with you again.
I want to say I think you were destined
to be together, the picture proves it.

for Taylor and Julia

The Miracle Worker

On the shoulder, on all fours
on the potholed county road, clawed
near death by the indignity of people
bound determined to not listen
no matter how many mandates you issue,
you wobble, wounded company man
miles from your cubicle
on the ground floor of the squat
office complex, and howl,
deep-seated, sourceless, existentialist
tears boiling up into a drenching
flood in the field ahead
where cows, upright and unruffled,
shimmer on the edge of sight.
You didn't know you had it in you

but now you are lighter, look,
on your feet and striding,
the day a lighter shade of slate,
the trees a darker green,
and a limo slows and sweeps you up—
later, awake, you remember
back in the field you mouthed
I hope the cows will be all right—
and you're ascending in a jagged diagonal,
riding away from and rising above
the water you've just let loose,
the flat land you've left behind,
broken white lines whizzing by, and where

this limo which is really a helicopter is headed
is anybody's guess.

Three Storms

1

Our oldest dog was an oak.
Ate everything we fed her and a lot we didn't.
Burst first out the door
to keep the neighbor dogs in their place.
Storms rolled through and she was inconsolable.
Followed us from room to room.
Panted. Paced. Burrowed the throw rug
wearing a weirdly ecstatic face.
The doggie rapture? We couldn't be sure.

It was a wet, portentous summer.
Trees fell eight hours apart
at opposite ends of the street.
Every morning another roach belly-up in the study.
We ordered her a thundershirt.
The name sounded great: chain mail,
suit of armor, happy place,
pliable yet inviolable.
The idea was we were to wrap her up
snug as a sausage; the pressure
would work its magic.

One night the power went out.
We played backgammon by candlelight
until I grew tired of rolling the dice.
A last pass at our phones, and to bed.
Looked out at the flash-bulb sky,
heard the thunder roll into itself.
Shuddered. Drew into each other.
Sweated through our separate dreams.

The dog snored,
blissful inside her shirt-shield.

2

      Roughing it.
Rain tapping for two straight days
           our pop-up camper,

      fog shrouding ground.
Flu-ridden, under a quilt,
         I've seen nothing

    of the other family
we're camping with:
          father who works with mine,

    soft-spoken mother,
snooty daughter
        I sort of but don't much

    know from school, or want to.
Lukewarm bath-air,
        my stomach straddling

    full and hungry,
little TV making
        the hollows of Dad's cheeks

    glow with advertisements—
tires, power tools,
        knives so sharp they could cut

    silence. My head is hot.
Mom slides the cold thermometer
        under my tongue:

       ninety-nine and holding.
She floats the theory
            of leaving early. No response.

      Pop tab hiss, cola cracking ice.
The other father and his daughter
           climb down from their camper

     in raingear, disappear
down a trail. We're here
           until the bitter end.

       A sick miracle
how this is understood
           without being said aloud—

     suck it up, ride it out.
Mom flips on the burner,
           flings pasta into the pot,

     is traveling somewhere
I can only imagine.
           In the wet mesh window

     between me and the elements,
I trace my name:
           first and last, all caps.

3

How this man in camouflage manages
to make it out the convenience store door
holding an extra-large cappuccino
and a paper-sacked twelve-pack of beer
and an opened umbrella over himself
in this Biblical rain and this night
like the inside of a silo,
walk into headlights' blear,
bluetooth in his ear, speak soothing syllables
to his wife or his child or someone else close
and in need of advice, and know
exactly in what corner of his pocket
the keyless remote is lodged, fumble for and find it,
and press unlock without having to look
escapes me. I text my wife:
If it's right to say these clouds are brewing,
imperial stout shall gush from the great heavenly tap.
No reply. *I wish you were here with me.* Smiley face.
The man eases his purchase onto the back seat,
takes his place behind the wheel, turns the key,
rifles his glove box for the right CD,
slides it into the slot, and takes off.

In Your Eggshell Dream

"I let you close once and what happens?
The floor's cut up in this one corner
and something in the ceiling is redolent of Death!
You forgot to put out more cans of air!
The curlicue-and-shrink-wrap shipment
continues to be unopened! And funny—
we sold no folderol last night
but now somehow we're out?
What is this, your personal treehouse?
When I get back with my large triple
chocolate chunk caramel skim latte,
I'd better see some evidence
I'm not dreaming!" But he is. He's been
assistant manager too long
or humble not long enough
or the trees have shriveled in the record heat
or a million other possible tropes.
You, you're no trope. You throw open the doors.
In marches a skeleton holding a handbag,
demanding a refund. You handle it.
The skeleton blows you a kiss and skips out.
In a minute which seems an hour
you take back a beaten guitar,
scuffed sneakers, driftwood, a Christmas tree,
someone's great-grandmother's butter knives.
You take a whiff of fresh Sharpie
and mark everything down
to two-seventy-nine. The phone keeps ringing
some jingle about redemption.
You poke your head outside

expecting the curb. You get the inside
of another store: eggshell walls,
empty shelves. One foot follows
the other across the threshold.
Windows without sale flyers—
endcaps without mouse pads or batteries—
register swaddled in plastic—
counter pristine as the dash of a Cadillac.
A store with nothing to sell—
your breath the only air.
Two orderlies muscle in, strap you into
a gurney, push you through a portal
to a clearing, a meeting
of guidance counselors. In the dancing
shadows of campfire flames
they sign rapidly and with much agitation.
In their shoulders hunches
a hushed, indeterminate fear,
which is what you hear
when you wake to the sports talk station rant
and slam the snooze button.
Your forehead glistens.
Once you were pretty good at stopping
your dreams on a dime.

Our Twenties

An awful time, honestly,
        a holding pattern—look at us there

so bored, my co-workers and me
        chugging the cheap stuff,

watching some band from Tampa
        ride hard their minor hit,

the one about wanting
        a trip-free life. No shit,

don't we all, bless us every one.
        Bless my ex, there

at the end of the table
        with her new boyfriend

none of us have met,
        who barely looks legal, and notice

I don't say anything, I'm trying
        to hitch myself to the train.

Bless, I guess, the singer
        shaking his dirty blond locks,

trying to save the scene
        by personality, suddenly

boogieing next to us,
        microphone with the longest cord

plugged into the secret
        most of us could use,

band vamping, bless stale smoke,
        bless beer-sour stench.

He stops at my face, my failure
        to smile, cracks a joke

the punch line of which
        is *Penthouse*. Boo me maybe

for not playing along.
        But look how I hold the moment.

The bassist's note choked,
        the jukebox locked in rainbow,

everyone stoked
        to see who will move whom.

Bless the exit I blast through
        so hard it hurts,

never mind it's freezing
        and I've left my coat in there

or the two guys I've known the longest
        are tearing down the street

trying to talk me back. Bless them.
        Forgive me for thinking

as I hunch into the cold *too bad*,
        that one song is really something.

The oncologist, hand on the doorknob,

one foot turned to you, one toward Florida.
        Purple socks, stethoscope

like a divining rod, tie tending left.
        You with your unanswerable questions,

he with his Kilimanjaro of charts,
        wearing the weariness of an oracle.

Hasn't warmed to the anecdote,
        hasn't let slip the unguarded moment,

doesn't figure to. Hates to speculate,
        not trained to serve hope.

Treads in narrow circles in which he is trusted.
        If in a ballroom filled with mercy

would walk out, unseduced.
        But not unsympathetic, not deaf.

You have something of a shared history,
        he with his training, you

with your feelings ready to rip.
        In another guise, with some goosing,

he could pull you out of the pool
        where you've been treading water

so long, drape a towel
        over your quivering shoulders.

New Glasses

The dog stands still but is sloping to the right.
The crabapple sapling bends like a headstone.
He wishes to send his bifocals over the fence.
Seeing is no longer a feather on the cheek.

The head and neck have muscled in.
Up just so to read the ants on the steps.
Down just so to read the new wife next door.
Ground no longer where he plants his feet.

He can't play two saxophones at once,
dredge harmony from some quarry.
He has to really sit still,
admit that light might, here on out, be stained.

Windows glow up and down the block.
Neighbor kids shoot hoops by floodlight.
Rubber thump on pavement, scuffle of soles.
Dusk disappearing. He slips into sound.

II

Thesis

Nothing to say and I'd said it
    again and again over eighty pages.
On the quad, oaks in rows, in shadow.
    I untangled myself, left the carrel,
wobbled into winter a little crazed,
    breath-vapor breaking, drove somewhere
I'd never been and even now can't
    tell you where it was, some clearing,
some place to make myself disappear.
    The moon glared like a flashlight;
skeletons of trees, frostbitten leaves.
    One question crashed into the next.
Why was I here? Why couldn't I
    hunker down, try harder, punch through?
What if I couldn't? In a dream I'd been
    pressed between hard covers,
glued and shoved onto a high shelf
    still speaking. What was I thinking?
Where would I go? I stared at nothing
    until I could tell myself I could,
until the cold was deep inside me.

Chemo

1

Five-pill rainbow at high noon.
Pink pockets of rash. Someone
is tapping my head with a tiny mallet
and trampolining my stomach.
Alien-child pallor, fallen-out hair—
it could be worse. First time,
it was. This time I ride
home over surface streets.
A wasp loops a figure eight
on the stoop. A weed whacker
buzzes through a curtain of kudzu.
I can burrow among books,
dote on my dogs. I can mothball
the memory of my just-finished drip
in the unlit corner of the mind-closet.
Safe zone. Dark solid doors.
Latter-day Dylan and headphones.

But dial it back, please, cult
of the half-full glass. You don't
know prednisone like I do.
I'm fascinated by my outstretched hand.
I jitterbug while lying still.
The living room is a tilt-a-whirl come true.
The wine country map on the wall
wavers. The coffee table angles.
I hold the handrail, write a wobbly script,
can stand being sick but not weak,

can't understand hungry and queasy
at once. The stove hisses like a snake.

My wife stirs meatballs. Bless her heart.
My taste buds have moved to Mars.
Chicken is salted rubber, egg salad
insufferable. Give me that engineered shit.
Mac and cheese from a cardboard box.
Meat from a can. Applesauce with a straw.
Open that Coke, love,
hand me the whole bottle. I'm hot.
I find myself likely
to punch someone's lights out.

2

Rank rises in my nostrils,
unbidden, unpinnable.
Burnt popcorn and banana peel.
Nail polish. Cut lumber.
Pine needles steeping in isopropyl.
Day-old mown grass in a tied-off bag
on a curb in the code-orange heat
and chocolate pudding have had a child.

Flashback-shudder. Mind-rewind
to the previous helplessness.
Agoraphobic. Homesick.
Laminar-flow air-whoosh
isolation chamber. Out the window
the tree-lined streets of Wauwatosa.
Me in bed, on my back, eager
for the churning to stop.
Hickman hooked into five
toxic, crisscrossing rivers.

Mom and Dad scrubbing their hands,
rubber-banding masks over their mouths
before they speak. Not much to say.
Hemoglobin, hematocrit, platelets.
Licorice lozenges, empty Sprite,
orange Jello, lukewarm soup,
tape player, upchuck bin.
But wait. How dare I almost forget
my brother, my donor,
my almost-perfect match
four floors below, gone under,

flat on a metal table,
long needle in his hip?

3

NBA pregame: Sager paces
the sideline in his lime green suit,
far gaunter than me, holding for dear life
his mic. Fear folded.
Lines deep in his forehead. Nose like a beak.
If I cut myself, I might die. Only half-joking.
How he seems to really care
what the point guard has to say.
How evenly he nods.
Twenty-some bone marrow biopsies,
twenty-some sessions of chemo,
two transplants—he has stared down the barrel
and re-entered the arena.

Lord, let me only live up to that.
Let no one catch me languishing
here in the basement, blanketed, sunk into the sofa,
hooked into the reality TV feed,
riding out, not rising above, the bumps.
Pills arrayed on the TV tray—
one to make me spacy,
four to bring me back safely.

for Jason Jewell

The Mirage

You and your new friends in a leather booth
inside a giant chandelier. Fancy blazers and ties.
From here you see it. All the losing
is downstairs. This smell, you smell it
consistently in this hotel—
the perfume of disappointment,
sicklier than car freshener, stronger than Lysol.
The menu is pink watercolor
on parchment. Everything is in Sanskrit.
Your server thrusts her fists in victory
and says they're out of food
except for the popcorn and the watercress
but she can bring drinks
until the cows come home.
The tall one in your party crawls
under the table, toots his noisemaker.
You rise and excuse yourself.
The bathroom mirror beams back
a rhinoceros in a pond. On the way out
you're given a Blood and Sand
on the rocks. You are in the middle
of ranks of roll-stepping soldiers,
rigid in camouflage, gripping
their rifles close to their faces,
marching to the same silent anthem.
It takes but a second for you to fall in line.

In the Lobby of the Women's Residence

It was as though she didn't remember
we'd been in the same classes together

or I'd helped her write three fourths of her thesis
or we'd driven to California and back

or fought like dogs, or I'd entertained
the thought of stranding her in Texas

even as I was past anxious for us to fuck
and put whatever this was

behind us, or that we'd taken
more than a few photos of one another,

some unwittingly sexy,
or the ones of her I was thinking of

were making me crazy. But she had to;
we'd done that, then not. We were seated

at either end of a long sea-green sofa,
just her hunched into herself, arms crossed,

just my hands clasped in my lap.
Her editing gig hadn't panned out,

but not to worry, she said,
she was getting by. Living

in this monument to morality
suited her: affordable, gated,

other women sitting in high-backed chairs
sharing news softly, so as not to be shushed.

She got up, apologized,
said she just wasn't herself tonight.

We hugged like distant cousins,
made vague plans: maybe Sunday,

maybe the Statue or a gallery.
The elevator swallowed her. I made myself

stay, watch the pastel walls,
listen to the time chiming.

Harbor Island

Farther down the beach,
kids chase each other into the waves.
A kite is puffed up by the wind. Twilight,
high tide, hyperactive sea.
We ease Mom into the unfolded chair,
help her button her sweater. She grins
through the pain. No walker,
no cane, no wheelchair, not yet.
She's from a line who says it does no good to complain.
Tonight, tired, I agree.
In the surf, a heron sneaks up on dinner.
My wife and I wade in ankle-deep.
There is much to be said for this beach
that will never be said,
or if it will, by someone who lives here
year-round, who can say it
and forget it. I wish I had a shovel
to dig a bed and dream
the even-keeled dreams of the dead.
Farther down, kids fight
to keep the fire going. They fan, they blow.
Mom looks on from a body which has betrayed her
and in a low, flat murmur
says she could sure go for some lobster,
claws, shell, the good stuff, the kind you have to want
to work for.

In Your Flea Market Dream

Folklore. Cookbooks. The usual fruitcakes
and cookies. Pirated CDs
buttressing happy Buddhas.
Stray ax, busted shovel, forlorn rake
from a small failed reclamation.
One Jazz Age painting bleeds into the next.
Lungs, hearts, biceps,
miscellaneous tendons
in humming refrigerator cases.
A wigwam. A coal-black casket.
No prices. Everything for the taking.
No one taking and no one to say
you can't. An old man in overalls
is cussing people out for five bucks a pop.
The line winds outside the tent
through the park and doesn't end
until the monument
built for the men who gave themselves
for a forgotten cause. The heat
has bound your shirt to your chest.
In your right hand you've been bequeathed
a globe. You close your eyes and spin.
Your finger lands on Germany.
Down the line comes a country maid
giving mist-spritzes from a bottle. You alone
see it's really a harmonica,
you alone seize up at the wheeze
which reminds you of railroad tracks
and huge flies. You leapfrog
three states to the edge of a lake,

green to its bottom. Something
keeps you from jumping in.
Two boys reel in their lures. "Nothing biting,"
one chuckles. A joke you know
you've heard before.

Royal Caribbean

The mansion was center of the small island;
the island was center of the sea;
the sea took cues from the like-minded sky—

detached, immovable, cerulean.
From the lido deck of the luxury liner
we swirled sauvignon blanc in our tumblers

until we were tipsy from convincing ourselves
we lacked, had fallen short, gotten left behind.
The mansion chained the island to the mind.

Behind a fence, a gardener in a wide-brimmed hat
tended hyacinths and seemed to be chanting;
at his side, a Great Dane gnawed a toy bone.

We enjoyed the wine but had tasted better years.
We imagined ourselves important to the tableau.
We kept returning to his hands: moving, moving again.

Coupling

Much later, after the latest failure,
they curled up on the sofa and again
went over the options, each of which
he maintained would make him less of a man,
and she said no, they were like a plumber
come to fix the pipes and didn't he want
the pipes to work, and he said when
he was on top of her, thinking how keenly
he wanted to give her what she wanted
and he felt himself go soft, he figured
the only solution was a monastery
for him or a lover for her, or better yet
cut off his dick and be done with it,
the script, the whole groping after bliss,
and she said that wasn't what he wanted,
and he said no but in a way it was,
and she said life without a dick would be
opera, and he laughed, and after a while
they had said all they needed to or could
so they pressed closer and let the night
and the silence settle, nothing now but
the ticking fridge, the clatter and fall
of new ice, and in this way it became
not a hurdle but a puzzle, and in this way
it was decided they would try again.

The Saloon in the Side of the Mountain

is a hardscrabble affair,
a sawed-off, knotted tree-trunk half for a bar,
charred stumps for stools,
glazed gazes into the middle distance
for actual emotions. Sundown,
subfreezing, ten thousand feet up
in a stand of conifers, beer bottles
sheathed in accreting layers of ice
as is your general outlook on life.
The bartender, swaddled in a snowsuit,
lifts with mittened hands
a handle of vodka. For some time
he's obliged the bobcat to your right's
increasingly drunk and aesthetic orders—
something, sir, with a little astringency,
not too homey, yes, friendly
but efficient, something that will wave hello
but won't stand in my way—
while you've sulked and stuck to draft.
The dartboard nailed to the blasted aspen
is shredding, pockmarked with throws
errant and right on the nose.
Who plays darts at this altitude?
The ranger, the rare through-hiker,
the lonely proud coyote?
Enough for a team? A league?
Or just poor saps like you
who gave up aiming years ago?
Pretty good metaphor,
the bobcat whispers. And who is he,

impish grin, little ears, lopped-off
stub for a tail, padding in here,
sipping from a coupe, ruminating like you?
Does the wilderness get old, too?
Do all animals burn
for something better? Does it matter
that bobcats don't drink or speak
or that this one is asking you to dance?
Or that you've pushed back
from the sawed-off bar, found your feet
on the blanket of needles, wobbled
over to the jukebox (a jukebox
in the side of the mountain?), pushed
a quarter in and pressed Play?
Or that your hand has extended
to the bobcat, or that your brain
is popping in a million different places?

In Your Teaching Dream

You enter a hangar at the end of a landing strip
in a frosty midwestern field. You lay down
your scuffed satchel. Freezing in here.
A single light bulb burns 200 feet above.
A 777 casts a monster shadow.
Neon green flyer taped to the landing gear:
History of the Known Universe,
8:15 to 8:30 p.m., two nights a week. That's you.
Students dangle their skinny legs from the wings,
regarding you as a crow does a carcass.
Where are the mechanics with their instruments,
the pilots with their cocky postures?
You don't need much. A book,
some desks, a rolling whiteboard,
a pack of black markers, a megaphone,
a cop to get them down from there,
and content, you need some compelling content
and a compelling style, no bells
or bullshit, just honesty, just an honest solid stance.
The bulb sputters and dies.
The students whoop and wow and punch each other's arms.
The inability to see does not equal the inability to plan.
You feel in your satchel for a pen
and come out with a pistol. Your thumb is startled
yet soothed rubbing the nubbly grip.
Now you can really get something done.
8:15 p.m. The frost hardens in the field.
You nod and come out of your crouch.
Content and style, you start, *content laced with a little style.*

Into History

> *Let us all be from somewhere.*
> —Bob Hicok, "a primer"

I go home, grow closer
        to official sadness. Sams Gap,
Nolichucky, Happy Mart,
        half-abandoned mall,
rock-dotted pasture
        ringed by barbed wire,
box turtle smack in the center
        of a hairpin curve,
bass boat, man-made dam,
        teenagers chugging beer
by firelight, swearing
        they will not be bought,
left at the light, quick right
        into the old subdivision
built on sinkholes, my parents
        still in the same house
and sinking, concrete
        driveway where I learned
too late to ride a bike,
        learned a good jump shot
but never tried out, bedroom
        where I barged through scales,
heard notes but rarely
        the tune, living room,
second-hand smoke,
        kitchen of warmed-over
pork chops, anger choked
        but never dead, family room
where many late nights

   (everyone else was upstairs
dreaming) I snapped off lights,
   dispensed with clothes,
sneaked out into gathering
   storm, grass crackling,
breeze in the branches,
   wishing I could go somewhere,
really fuck something.

III

Eastman Meditations

1

Acrid, ammoniac, organic,
the stench of utility—
chemicals, fibers, plastics
being born, bubbling up
from vats, trial runs in tubs,
little labs—piecemeal victories,

happy accidents poured,
stored in black flecked barrels
(CAUTION, DANGER, HAZARD)
in windowless brick buildings,
small dark worlds—
things that go into other things,

things with half-seen half-lives—
shine in your knives,
sweet in your frosted flakes,
uniformly red meat
(please, eat),
glass impossible to break

or dissuade from its part—
compunctionless consumption,
one-God factory town—
from Stone Drive to Meadow Lane
thumps one heart,
one giant presumption,

tools a brown station wagon
to shoe store, playground,

pharmacy, market, and so on,
and so forth—cf.
Shangri-la, cf. milk and honey,
cf. the pudgy kid with the big round

head in the middle seat,
stomach satiate
yet desperately hungry,
nose wanting to vanquish
yet burn into memory
that smell of many dead fish.

2

Dad is practicing a talk for work.
Lights off and the slide projector fan
a warm, dry breath.
Mom and I are the warm bodies.
He talks with hands, talks above our heads,
talks white text on royal blue background,
talks facts, talks in a tone
meant to educate. Minutes
drone with a bee's exactitude.
He asks how he sounds. Mom says
everything he wants to hear.
I'd hate to be the people
he has to impress. I'm in third grade
and I don't know what he does.
He draws compounds with his mechanical pencil,
mixes things, makes cakes
from mysterious elements.
When he tries to explain,
my eyes drift up to a spider web,
down the spines of his college texts.
Once and only once do we see him in his office.
Green metal desk. Hard hat,
coveralls hanging from a coat rack,
binders bursting on a shelf,
phone with a row of unlit buttons.
Wednesday. Lunchtime. He has a meeting at one.
He unwraps his sandwich
and asks us if we're doing anything fun.
Probably. I don't remember. The summer is stalling
in a hamburger-and-milkshake haze.
I remember only that I am puzzled.

No pictures on the wall.
His Ph.D. in a dusty dime-store frame.
He says he plays bridge in the middle of the week
but the other offices are empty.
This is around the time I learn to swim.
I've never changed the music for this scene,
a grinding whine from outside:
proto-dynamos, pieces of neo-steel.

3

Smoke blacker than bombs
barrels blowing up every six seconds
steam screaming from pipes

> *harmful amounts may be absorbed through the skin*

Steel lintel ripped from door
Pinwheeling   severing
fleeing man's leg at the knee
and man continuing to flee

> *material can ignite without an ignition source*

Woman in business suit
darting around firemen
scaling ten-foot chain-link fence
dropping straight down on spiked heels
into melting street   her feet
slipping out of those prisons
holding her up into safety

> *may polymerize in the presence of heat*

Space station   holy land
picture postcard of higher purpose
if you look closely you can see
humpbacked door frame
sheared sill   hairline crack

> *reacts with water in a dangerous or unusual way*

Barely smell or sound
hard to believe bad ever happened

gas station down from the coal-gas tower
two men light cigarettes
next to a pallet of propane tanks

two million consecutive safe working hours

I see body parts in black trash bags
hush money   pavement
poured over dirty secrets

catches fire if exposed to air

In the library, a single
poker-faced paragraph about that day

who'd want to remember it anyway

Look
I worked there one summer
swept production floors
painted yellow curbs yellower
in winter got a call from my doctor
white cell count was sky-high

stand back until it burns itself out

4

In the days of tetherball and four-square,
when tempers flared or tears were shed,
there was rarely a teacher
who wouldn't walk over and settle us
with a hand on the shoulder
and say *it's just a game*,
a nice idea we didn't much believe
but filed away just in case
before we resumed one-upping one another.

I am on a bus with my family
and a passel of other Eastman people,
destination Neyland Stadium.
Every rung on the ladder is rowdy—
chemists to techs to operators,
Ph.Ds to dropouts.
Dad wears his sky-blue UCLA cap.
Brown bottles clink, boos sound,
off-color jokes about the West Coast
are passed around. Sticky
September air through the windows.
Mom looks as though she might melt.
Dad smirks, doesn't blink,
keeps one eye on the interstate.
His fandom is no less competitive.

But let it be said
he lords it over no one's head
after his alma mater not only beats
but shuts out the Volunteers.
Back on the bus it's night; exits flash past.

I wake up and we're in the parking lot
in front of medical,
where earlier we all met,
and let it be said the air is cooler
and Mom has held it together,
and if anyone here is still pissed or distraught
they have subsumed it in cigarettes,
contemplation of the fumbles,
the lazy coaching, the countless
ways they could have done it better.

for Mark Painter

5

George Eastman shot himself in the heart in 1932.
His note spoke volumes:
"My work is done. Why wait?"
Philanthropist *par excellence*,
avid traveler, lifelong bachelor.
The shy, retiring type,
the world's most anonymous millionaire.
He had a few suitors,
but none came close to the silence of a darkroom.
Opportunity was to be ridden hard.
We the people wanted proof that we were alive,
every birthday, every bug and beehive,
and he obliged—
the film, the camera,
the dawn of point and click.
But we had to send the whole kit and caboodle to him
if we wanted to own our moments.
He lent his share of chemicals to the Great War,
his name to a music school.
Kept quiet a bad back and a creeping depression.
Toward the end, gave to Tuskegee,
MIT, dental clinics, philharmonics
as though his wealth might bite him.
Bought up a chunk of land in east Tennessee.
Men logged it,
mules dragged the logs in wagons
and the wagons through the wilderness
becoming less and less itself,
and the wood fueled a fire some would say
radiates to this day.
But you're fishing for a story.

You want the man behind the mission,
not the mission.
I imagine him in his mansion
in the middle of Rochester
in the last stretch of a lavish dinner party.
The string quartet plays its last pizzicato,
everyone except him stuffed
and respectably drunk.
He excuses himself from the small talk,
the cigars and cognac,
satisfied to stand
cold sober on the landing
and let industry do his speaking.

6

Slime, watery slime,
two-foot-high puke-mucus ooze—
never mind how it might look

under a microscope, it's alive
and climbing my childhood home
fenceline to foundation,

lapping, slapping the giant oak,
marooning the swing set,
the barbecue, the tulips too

suffused with the stink
of oblivion—boiling clouds,
Dad in monkey suit

thigh-deep in the murk-sea
wagging his finger, denouncing
the powers that be—

they tossed out my expertise
built that motor anyway
just plowed ahead didn't think

of anything but the future's
sparkling teeth so here you go
the ecology gone to pot

the universe biting us in the butt
if I could just find my lecture notes
I'd remember how—and I'm trying

to muscle through the undertow
to where he wobbles, where I might be
finally of some use, fill buckets,

dig trenches—stooped stranger
with two college degrees
up to his shoulders in soup,

finger not wagging but trembling
in the direction of his azaleas,
mouth sloping at one corner

and at the other ramping up
his dead certainty—*robbery*
rape they're getting away look

 at the magnitude we need a map
a plan where's my pencil I mean
my slide rule I mean youth

Thrash

My brother and my father up in the attic
        flat on their backs in the dead of summer

ripping out insulation, inhaling heat,
        me sitting somewhere nicer

and far removed. In fall,
        both of them grunting and nudging

the air conditioner from the window,
        my father on the ladder

barking *be careful*, me downstairs
        watching dumb TV. My brother

under the Duster, fumbling for the oil plug,
        doing his best to not fuck up,

me sailing through senior year,
        not studying, saving myself for later.

Of course the fight would break out
        in a room where I wasn't, of course

it would spill into the yard: my brother,
        my father swinging and missing,

sometimes connecting, collars tearing,
        my mother and me rushing in to break it up,

my brother shaking and declaring
        he was only hired help.

I never saw them fight again,
        not like that. My father in the garage

hammering nails, my brother
        plugged into the stereo

with my father's headphones,
        air-drumming a song I didn't understand—

molten fury, no melody,
        hello and go to hell.

Autumn

The Friday football games are winding down.
The floodlight over the garage
is always shining for the bored boy

out with his friends,
skimming rocks across the lake
or sitting in someone's truck, tossing back
tallboys of mischief.

The cool descends, the floodlight widens
and begins this poem.
The childhood canoe
corrodes in the overgrown grass.
Indigo has been elbowed aside by midnight.

Even at this distance,
I can feel the cornerback slam
the receiver to the ground
out of bounds,
hear the gasp as the clock ticks zero.

What I Fell Into

Retention pond, seminar, exam room, line,
cross-talk, long week, long year, small fatal
nail in tire, turn lane, chains, prosecco,
don't know, my ass, good as gold, dead deer
on shoulder, advice, tongue-bite, ego-
stroke, sorry, rough chop, doesn't matter,
cracked tooth, something, fashion, hydrangea,
why not, neighbor shooting fireworks, past,
habit, surrender, pursed lips, minute
by minute, illusion, why, new illusion,
autocorrect, something else, dry eye.

The Class of '86

Only 40 or so of you here—
a puddle, a tiny cross-section—
at the brand-new hotel and conference center.
The old intimidation hard at work.
But everyone seems to be mouthing in unison
over their complimentary drinks
You're not alone and *Look how
we've been sprung from the yearbook.*
Cheerleaders chatting up band geeks.
The class president trading barbs with the girl—
woman—whose answers he used to copy.
You and the salutatorian
having a heart-to-heart about singing
or summer or something else that brings you joy.
Some have become their own bosses,
most haven't, but many still claim
the spaces they are standing in.
The women, dear God, have gotten only more gorgeous.
You run through infinite alternate scenarios.
David and Shane (so their badges claim)
shake someone's old pom-poms. The dust rises,
the insults land like smart bombs.
Nine takes to take the class picture.
You're most impressed with the one
in which only half of the now-30 of you
are smiling. Your hands curiously to yourself.
There are prizes:
youngest grandfather, most unrecognizable,
best posture, least beaten up by time…
The taco bar and the baked potato station go untouched.

A shout. Jello shots in the parking lot.
The playlist has changed from senior prom
to the heyday of the late and ignored
Curtis Mayfield, a voice before your time
and well ahead of his. You assume
your place in the circle of now-23 or -22,
you're losing count, but no sweat,
everyone is quiet and listening
to that falsetto like a balm. The still-new
moon is sneaking some beams
through the windows. You have the room
until midnight, and there's so much to say.

While Everyone Else Was Disappearing

Good Morning America faded into a station ID. The IV cart beeped. I unhooked, alcohol-wiped my catheter, shot saline through with a syringe. The tubing snapped like a matchstick. And that was all I needed: *what if the port gets infected? what if I have to go back in? what if they have to yank it out?* For the first time in months, I cried. My mother too. I ate another cinnamon roll; she poured more juice. "Let's see what the doctors say," she offered. In the bathroom mirror, my face a fleshy balloon.

No more waiting. I threw on my coat and blasted outside. Steel sky, spitting snow. Mittened children squealed down the slide into their parents' arms. Padlocked, drained pool; gray grass stubble; rosebushes holding their own. Sagging slabs of balcony. Sliding glass doors into others' mornings. At the tennis court gate, I banked a hard left down rows of taillights.

In that drab apartment, my mother, I was certain, was making a mountain of mac and cheese, both of us would eat more than we needed, and both of us would feel bad about it. Another lap around the complex. Another. Sweat dotted my forehead. My breath clouded. I wanted somebody to see me. I was a spinning firecracker, a gathering tornado.

Make It Easy on Yourself

The tape sits atop a stack of its ilk.
The case is black.
Underneath it, mixes from college,
K-tel collections, Sylvia Plath
spitting out hard-won syllables
in the last year of her life.

It isn't even mine. I swiped it from Dad's cabinet
after he'd gone to bed,
stuck it in my bag, brought it
here to my office five hours south
where it rests, where I don't dare listen.

The A & M Records A & R department
clearly didn't bust its budget here.
Burt Bacharach is a pensive, handsome detail.
No liner notes, nothing that would betray
love given, care taken, actual sweat—
just this dull gray cassette
with the factory-stamped song list.
Bacharach back then was much in demand
and demanded much in kind.

Now, of course, I have the longer view.
Thirty-five years ago: big headphones,
big foam pads making dents in my head.
Bacharach might have been a mighty arranger
but he had a moose of a voice.
Mostly a lot of baroque piano,
some harp, some backup singers.

Small-town suburb. Idle time out the wazoo.
Implacable oak holding down the yard.
Hide and seek with the sisters across the street.
Their parents fought in the open air.
And there was that time Dad smacked me from behind
and I cried from surprise.

Years before,
in the far superior '60s sunshine,
Dad drives up the 101 from L.A.
on a weekend, on his way
to be with the woman he will marry—
lecture notes prepped, check,
lab reports marked, check,
worries tucked in the trunk, check,
blue sky made bluer, richer
by the AM pop heartbreak vibe
of which our Mr. Bacharach was so much a part.

Maybe Dad even bobs his head a bit.
Maybe he thumps his thumb on the steering wheel.
Surely he must have an eye on
the future. Maybe
the future looks back at him and smiles.

First Friday

At the corner of Main and Maple, the man
brings his lemonade cart to a halt.
The women peer at each other's guitars and tune.
Cars crawl along the cottonwood square,
people queue at the funnel cake truck.
The potter arranges his work without a word,
the painter places landscapes
at her feet. Tables unfold
with the speed and purpose of swimmers.
Rolls of tickets lie ready to unfurl.
Another one of those clear, slow afternoons
pilfered from a postcard. The sun seems
as though it may never set.
And you, perched on your stool, in the cool
tasting room, lower your nose
inside the glass, catalog
the small triumphs and ineffable satisfactions.
This vine is 125 years old.
For roughly the 125th time today
you wish you had something intelligent to say
about how the color spreads
to the edges, how the wine reminds you
of nothing but gets you the closest to zen
you'll ever be. In some nightmares
you try to fight your way out of a vat
of pudding, or run from a gun, or come back
to this same stretch of property
just to discover the women have gone, given up
music for good. What have you done
to merit this scene so close to the real thing?

(Note, too, the server seems to like you
and has poured you another splash.)
Your mind no longer monkey but some grand bird
high over a canyon, not even needing wings.

IV

On the Rapids

Not until we were back in the cabin
with the rented view of the mountains,
after dinner, dried off
and sunk with wine, not until
we had found our way to the porch swing
and heard the crickets taking over
could I begin to appreciate
our raft hung up between two jutting rocks,
us flailing, yelling for help,
me feeling like a tree
struck by lightning, stripped of its bark,
how I feared some local patrol would find us
belly-up, crows descended
and having a party in our intestines.
Not until we were not talking, not until
we heard the river hewing
to its relentless purpose,
was I finally impressed. How like a champ
she clambered out of the raft
and unsnagged us, and how I knew
I had to dig that paddle in
and how undramatically
we slid back into the current,
down another mile to the takeout—
slick banks, unrelieved greenery,
pinpricks of sunlight flashing on the surface.

Franklin County Lowdown

1

Walking along the tracks, feeling haughty,
      snarky, eager to fling my angsty matter

at the nearest target—right here, early Christmas:
      double-wide, potbellied man on the porch

yelling at someone inside, bending over
      a crumpled bike—I catch myself mumbling

if this place were to go up it would not be missed.
      Skip a year, I'm in front of the former

trailer now shell, black chimney,
      faint smoke, coda—arson? lit cigarette?—

anyway gone, downgraded to history,
      flash of guilt—did I wish it? No, insists

my better self, that's over, you're in better
      spirits, committed to the greater effort,

a page a day for every day you're here.
      I leave a day early. Year later, same spot,

ashes gone, paved patch, woods beyond, woman
      poking at her phone. My point—the lot sits

across the street from the fire department.

2

Coat buttoned to my chin,
I walk the loop
around the ghosts of children—
monkey bars, rocking horse,
headstone for the old grade school,
buried echo of a bell. A caboose
rusts on the rusting tracks.
The church and cemetery sink invisibly.
The dollar store clings to solid ground.
Rarely another parked car,
only the occasional wanderer.

Yet there are stirrings. The sun
stares through the cloud-mask.
A cardinal flits into the frame
and alights on a weathervane.
The grass has been trimmed within an inch of the earth.
Gardener, architect, are you here?
I thank you.
I have failed to separate myself
from the need to speak.

Second Act

Blevins, back at the brook,
back in his childhood home

propped on cinder blocks,
backyard with kudzu-covered hole,

bought for a song, bought for saving
but Blevins would say for the first time

he's thriving. The day apt:
coffee black, toast light,

clouds rolling back, rocking chair
rocking with his measured breathing,

front porch freshly painted,
freshly emptied beanbag ashtray

atop the wicker table
though the urge to smoke

has dissipated. He shifts,
narrows his eyes, some rustle

out there, deer probably
but he's holding out for ghosts—

mother hanging shirts, brother laughing
HEY from inside the outhouse.

Puzzle pieces. Wife who left him
overnight for another,

son who fled to the other side
of the world, factories,

mills, money he could never master.
Temper. Talking over others,

ripping up friendships. Baseball bat
taken to that poor sap's lamp.

The nut in the stomach, the sense
things would keep eroding

no matter what fad found
itself in power. Summer:

the Gulf, tide creeping up,
how he swore it was coming

straight for him. Beautiful kids
tossing football, gulls swarming

over sand. Blevins, cautious
of too much plot. Sees not

story but wisps of cotton.
Stopped fighting, stopped expecting,

can't say how but started
returning. Makes note of the break

in the weather. Days like this
feels strong enough to throw

a boulder through it. Two boys
shamble up the hill to the bus stop,

eyes glued to their phones,
laughing in tandem, backpacks

crammed full. He furrows his brow.
Still working on it. Can't admit them

into his heart as he can
his hand around a ratchet.

Knows gears. Knows how to fix
fears about fuse boxes

and will, without complaint,
unclog gutters, putty gaps,

pull weeds, feed pets. Nothing,
Blevins, if not creature

of routine, man of one sock
then the other sock, calls the dog,

feels good to plod down steps
onto flagstone, pine bark path

winding back into old growth.
Bends his ear to the tanager's burr.

Tiny creek. Tobacco patch
lining the other side. Fingers

touching every trunk, tongue
tasting the wet iron breeze,

same breeze that carried him away,
that brought him back, deep,

deeper into the waking dream.

Letter to Ferris from Decatur

Jim: Rare fog today. The backlit trees guard their secrets.
Leaves dangle from branches like ornaments. Seems
Hopkins was right—the world is charged. I don't want
to write another word about not being able to write.
Toledo treats you well, I trust. Is life still full?
I'm still doing the work I was meant to do, still
brushing scales from my students' eyes. I like it.
Of course I enjoy myself more when I can sit here,
look out the window, read meaning into the rain-sheen.
Me and my little poem-moments. Pain is hard to do
justice to. One of many reasons I am in awe of you.
I live on a blue island in a sea of red. Progressive.
Seductive. Bring me a lager, please, on a pub patio;
that's my kind of policy. Like our last meeting
in Chinatown, the Evergreen, that old-school place
beneath the moan of the Stevenson. It was cold.
We were tired and overstimulated by the conference.
You recommended a book; we tossed around the concept
of fame a few minutes. *Thank God for anonymity*, you said.
Scrape of silverware, passing of platters. I nodded.
How different my life if I were Bukowski-loud,
Ginsberg-garrulous? But the night was also charged
with silent, eloquent gestures: our server's tiny smile,
iridescent fish cutting clean angles in the water. Jim,
I wish to swim with that much purpose. We ate;
we paid. We walked across Wentworth to your car,
went to the keynote, sat in the back, applauded.
Anonymity: I hear you, but I have to think about it.

In Your Teaching Dream

You attach yourself to a cardinal's wing
and touch down outside
this building at the edge of town,
once sexy, now echoey,
painted beige and carpeted,
a place for hawking cars or autographs.
There's Barbara still behind the desk
fielding calls. The wastebaskets brim
and the dust motes float. There's Taylor
leading a tour group. You tag along.
You hurry past empty conference rooms,
a water fountain on the fritz. You shiver.
The heat hasn't been on in years.
A dog scuttles by with a rabbit in its teeth.
There's an agenda. There's no time to ask
Taylor, why a tour group, you work here,
you have a master's. You tiptoe around
a prayer circle. Heads are down, humming.
You're led into a bunker of office chairs
still in boxes. A spinning disco ball
is the only light. No one has any questions.
You run to a gap in the cinder-block wall.
Verdure in four directions, a horse
behind a fence. It's eternity
before you remember you worked here too
and maybe still do.
Taylor hands you a coffee mug and a spoon.

Trash Duty

In the twilight of another dinner party at Derek's
I rose from my place and thought *what a night,
what a lovely thing*, and I was floating
up to just below the crown molding,
looking down on Daniel shepherding the china
into the kitchen, Deidre scraping and rinsing,
Darcy stacking the dishwasher, and it was lovely
how easy the laughter, how simple the fact
I was also looking at myself and for once
not feeling disgusted, so untroubling the dust
bunnies in the corners, the hairline crack
zigzagging along the wall, I didn't mind
when Dawn said *ice cream* and everyone oohed,
that was my cue, back down, drunk just enough
to double-knot the straps on the first try,
walk down the chipped, crumbling steps
and drop the bag, nearly bursting with bones
and scraps of salad, into the behemoth bin
which tomorrow would be grabbed and emptied
by the long arm on the yellow truck. Tomorrow
I would be back to renting my body. Tonight
was the thing, tonight was *it*. It was cool
and dry for late July, the stars seemed to be
studying me lightly swaying in the driveway.

Three-Mushroom Tart, Dayton, Oregon

      How to do right by dirt,
transliterate loam, foggy dawn,
            damp hillside, the plot, the planet,

      the enormity? How to bake it
beneath fragile, flaky layers,
            control heat, calibrate

      magnificence, how properly
praise this wedge of heaven
            on its pristine plate, balanced

      on the palm of the server
serving us all? Now is it set
            in front of me, now I see it,

      nose, mouth, tongue, thus
brain, where it will burn
            permanently, where earth and rain

      and recall will remain perfect.
Love is like mushrooms. Why not?
            Why not us at this soft-lit table

      in this refurbished restaurant
of the mind, stunned a little
            at the sight? But enough, love.

      How does it taste? Like my life.
Like ours. Before you or me,
            before anyone, way back, before beginning.

Remission

The number one song was "Don't Worry, Be Happy."
Everywhere. In crevices and creeks.
Tire-flattened, but alive.
Me, riding to clinic
absent-minded, outpatient high,
reading nothing into the potholed pavement,
majoring in undecided.
Steve Goeller, friend,
inpatient yet again,
sat in the cramped waiting room and stared straight ahead.
Fever spiking, white count wavering,
he let it be known
he hated that song, its fake-reggae bleached-bland
sentiment, its simplicity.
Don't worry, be happy. Really.
His wife's laughter boomed, filled the whole unit.
She trash-talked Steve's numbers,
talked up the docs, talked to strangers,
could have won over the walls.
He didn't agree or not,
didn't curse or lash out, just wore the face
of a man who could no longer be surprised.
Bobby McFerrin singing rings around himself
a cappella. Another day at the office.
First release, flopped.
Second release, shot up like a rocket.
I had the CD. Simple pleasures,
silo in which to stockpile belief.
I know it made Mom feel much better
to sit with me. In no time

we were down in the lobby and out the door,
a centimeter closer to wellness.
Goodbye to Grover the parking lot attendant,
hello Pontiac, hello traffic,
left on Wisconsin, weighing dinner options,
right on 27th, over the little bridge—
don't worry—past the big brewery
and there turning to inhale—
be happy—the heady ferment of bread.

Two Raptures

1

If I stepped out of my body I would break
into a dead run, and I do, barefoot,

suddenly and strangely naked,
down the deck steps, over the jutting rocks

and almost total absence of grass—
it's a yard for dogs—and there she is,

latte streak against the still-sleeping weeds,
sniffing around the fence-edge,

considering the bricks, tilting her head at me—
my arms shorten to forelegs,

hands shrink to paws, nose now
a formidable and sensitive snout,

and just above where my butt once cleaved
sprouts a rascally tail

wagging furious loop-de-loops
in the not-yet-dawn, she and I

bound by the same boundless code,
digging up the bones of years,

barking in harmony at the garbage truck,
leaping at all small moving things.

2

For I will consider my three-legged dog Berkeley.
For she has lived a full cheese-block-eating, coffee-slurping, floor-licking life.
For she has barged through to sixteen, and barges on.
For she is a conductor of deep feeling.
For she was once four-legged but cancer bloomed.
For she can pant.
For she drinks much water and would drink, I declare, the breadth and depth of the river.
For she has the softest head.
For I scratch behind her ears and believe I have it figured out.
For I find solace in her white muzzle.
For it is the muzzle of the holy spirit.
For I know deep down she is a saint, and seeks the same.
For I have made for her a mighty resumé.
For she has skills: doctor, chef, advice columnist, meteorologist.
For no one can say she is not in constant pursuit.
For she tears into her senior food with the gusto of a puppy.
For I need not set an alarm.
For there is a thump like thunder from under the bed, and I pull her out and make it possible for her to stand.
For she is the dog I have always wanted to be.
For love is entwined with impatience and anxiety.
For when she is pacing and unsettled, I would give my leg for her to tell me what she wants.
For we give her much for what we presume is pain.
For she tests the stairs before she commits; here she is, hopping up, and I swear she is smiling.
For she wants only to be near.
For of course she has every right to smile.

For she follows me into the study, lies on her bed, and studies me.

For this is a house of counsel and consolation.

For in the backyard I stand guard as she scouts out the best place to conduct her business.

For I clean her up when she leaks.

For I shall fill her water bowl until the river runs dry.

Repair

cold-cocked by luck   me at my desk
      circling the word that will solve

everything   coffee
      gone cold   music cranked

no bed of roses   *no pleasure cruise*
      sealed inside the sound   I'd forgotten

warm winter   upper-arm pain
      X-ray   widened eyes

feathered bone   undefined mass
      three weeks and one doctor later

cut out   while he had me there
      laid out on the table   amenable

cut out another bump   benign
      in doing   cut a chunk of nerve

I survey the potholed street
      tap my palm   sparks dance

scar losing color   texture   almost forgotten
      cancer   you cartoon

you unsolicited gift   you will not be
      reborn   blossom into a system

look at me   breathing   dug out
      tunnel sealed   you made me special

friends' hands on my shoulder
      low voices   all the applesauce I wanted

now I'm myself again
      as close as I ever get   I'm sorry

you had to go   too much in front of me
      sun through window   waxwings chirping

urging   we're done here
      die already

I woke up and I was a comforter

with stitched bears and stenciled message
on a white backdrop
on top of a red bedspread

on a bed
in the basement of a cabin
at the end of the gravel road
in soft December rain.

Out back,
the deer inching down the hill, chewing shoots,
the robin pecking the ground
might have had it pretty good,

whatever. I was the clear winner.
Wood paneling,
the click of something settling.

No longer did I need
to feel important.
Stretched to all four corners of the bed

I was. I could lie
months, lifetimes

and know someone would soon pull me
close to herself, willingly.

Notes

Epigraphs:

Mark Halliday, from "Skein," in *Keep This Forever* (Tupelo, 2008); Diane Seuss, from "[There is a force that breaks the body]," in *Frank: Sonnets* (Graywolf, 2021).

"Chemo," section 3:

Craig Sager was a TV sports reporter and commentator who fought a lengthy, remarkable battle with leukemia.

"Eastman Meditations":

Section 3 reimagines the October 4, 1960 aniline plant explosion at Tennessee Eastman Company, Kingsport, Tennessee, which killed 16 and injured hundreds more. Some italicized lines are taken directly from the National Fire Protection Association's "hazard diamond" chart. Inspiration is also drawn from Pete Dykes's book *The Eastman Explosion Tragedy* and TEC engineer Pete Lodal's presentation. Thanks to Eric Diebert, who provided me access to the presentation.

Section 5 is informed by Elizabeth Brayer's invaluable *George Eastman: A Biography* (University Press of Rochester, 2011).

"Make It Easy on Yourself":

Written by Burt Bacharach and Hal David, a hit for Jerry Butler in 1962 and the Walker Brothers in 1965; also the title of the 1969 Bacharach album which the poem references.

"Two Raptures":

Section 1's first line is from James Wright's "A Blessing." Section 2's cadence and inspiration are drawn from Christopher Smart's *Jubilate Agno*.

Acknowledgments

Thanks to these journals in which the following poems first appeared, sometimes in different forms:

Another Chicago Magazine: "Our Twenties," "Into History," "Thrash"
The Comstock Review: "New Glasses"
Dead Mule School of Southern Literature: "Three Storms" (2), "In Your Eggshell Dream," "Harbor Island"
Drafthorse: "Eastman Meditations" (2, 3, 5)
Free State Review: "On the Rapids"
Flycatcher: "Franklin County Lowdown" (2)
Iodine Poetry Journal: "In Your Teaching Dream" ("Twenty-two students…")
jmww: "The Mirage," "In the Lobby of the Women's Residence," "The Class of '86," "Remission," "Two Raptures"
Kentucky Review: "Marriage"
Medical Literary Messenger: "Chemo"
Muse /A: "The Miracle Worker," "In Your Flea Market Dream," "Make It Easy on Yourself"
New Haven Review: "Trash Duty"
Pembroke Magazine: "Jazzercise"
Steel Toe Review: "Letter to Ferris from Decatur"
Tusculum Review: "The Saloon in the Side of the Mountain"
Wild Goose Poetry Review: "Coupling"

"Letter to Ferris from Decatur" also appears in *Stone, River, Sky: An Anthology of Georgia Poems*, edited by Carey Scott Wilkerson and Melissa Dickson (Negative Capability, 2015). "Three-Mushroom Tart, Dayton, Oregon" also appears in *The Reach of Song 2021*, published by the Georgia Poetry Society. "New Glasses" was read on episode 5 of the podcast *Secret Architecture: The Process of Process* (Staibdance, 2020).

For their generosity and thoughtful reading, special thanks to Keith Badowski, Katie Chaple, Liz Garcia, Travis Denton, Matthew Layne, Barry Marks, Marissa McNamara, and Steven Shields. Thanks also to the Bowers House in Canon, Georgia for needed time and space.

To my wife Rosalind, as always, my undying love and gratitude.

This book is dedicated to the memory of my mother Betsy; to my father Curtis and my brother Eric; and to all my families, near and far.

About the Author

Michael Diebert, a native of Kingsport, Tennessee, is the author of *Life Outside the Set*. He teaches writing, research, and literature at Perimeter College, Georgia State University and previously served as poetry editor of *The Chattahoochee Review* and president of Georgia Poetry Society. His poems have appeared on the podcast *Secret Architecture: The Process of Process* and in the zine *Not My Small Diary*. A two-time cancer survivor, Michael lives in Avondale Estates, Georgia with his wife and dogs.

Our Mission

BRICK ROAD POETRY PRESS

The mission of Brick Road Poetry Press is to publish and promote poetry that entertains, amuses, edifies, and surprises a wide audience of appreciative readers. We are not qualified to judge who deserves to be published, so we concentrate on publishing what we enjoy. Our preference is for poetry geared toward dramatizing the human experience in language rich with sensory image and metaphor, recognizing that poetry can be, at one and the same time, both familiar as the perspiration of daily labor and as outrageous as a carnival sideshow.

Available from Brick Road Poetry Press

www.brickroadpoetrypress.com

All These Hungers by Rick Mulkey

Escape Envy by Ace Boggess

My Father Should Die in Winter by Barry Marks

The Return of the Naked Man by Robert Tremmel

Face Cut Out for Locket by Jenn Blair

Available from Brick Road Poetry Press

www.brickroadpoetrypress.com

The Word in Edgewise by Sean M. Conrey

Household Inventory by Connie Jordan Green

Practice by Richard M. Berlin

A Meal Like That by Albert Garcia

Cracker Sonnets by Amy Wright

Things Seen by Joseph Stanton

Battle Sleep by Shannon Tate Jonas

Lauren Bacall Shares a Limousine by Susan J. Erickson

Ambushing Water by Danielle Hanson

Having and Keeping by David Watts

Assisted Living by Erin Murphy

Credo by Steve McDonald

The Deer's Bandanna by David Oates

Creation Story by Steven Owen Shields

Touring the Shadow Factory by Gary Stein

American Mythology by Raphael Kosek

Waxing the Dents by Daniel Edward Moore

Speaking Parts by Beth Ruscio

Also Available from Brick Road Poetry Press

www.brickroadpoetrypress.com

Dancing on the Rim by Clela Reed

Possible Crocodiles by Barry Marks

Pain Diary by Joseph D. Reich

Otherness by M. Ayodele Heath

Drunken Robins by David Oates

Damnatio Memoriae by Michael Meyerhofer

Lotus Buffet by Rupert Fike

The Melancholy MBA by Richard Donnelly

Two-Star General by Grey Held

Chosen by Toni Thomas

Etch and Blur by Jamie Thomas

Water-Rites by Ann E. Michael

Bad Behavior by Michael Steffen

Tracing the Lines by Susanna Lang

Rising to the Rim by Carol Tyx

Treading Water with God by Veronica Badowski

Rich Man's Son by Ron Self

Just Drive by Robert Cooperman

The Alp at the End of My Street by Gary Leising

About the Prize

The Brick Road Poetry Prize, established in 2010, is awarded annually for the best book-length poetry manuscript. Entries are accepted August 1st through November 1st. The winner receives $1000 and publication. For details on our preferences and the complete submission guidelines, please visit our website at www.brickroadpoetrypress.com.

Winners of the Brick Road Poetry Prize

2019
Return of the Naked Man by Robert Tremmel

2018
Speaking Parts by Beth Ruscio

2017
Touring the Shadow Factory by Gary Stein

2016
Assisted Living by Erin Murphy

2015
Lauren Bacall Shares a Limousine by Susan J. Erickson

2014
Battle Sleep by Shannon Tate Jonas

2013
Household Inventory by Connie Jordan Green

2012
The Alp at the End of My Street by Gary Leising

2011
Bad Behavior by Michael Steffen

2010
Damnatio Memoriae by Michael Meyerhofer

www.ingramcontent.com/pod-product-compliance
Lightning Source LLC
Chambersburg PA
CBHW021012090426
42738CB00007B/768